# Married to Self Love:

# Keep the Balance

## By:

### Kendrea Robinson, FNP-C

# Copyright

All rights reserved. No part of this publication may be reproduced, stored in a retrieval system, or transmitted in any form or by any means, electronic, mechanical, photocopying, recording, or otherwise, without written permission of the copyright owner

ISBN 978-0-578-76008-7 (paperback edition)
ISBN 978-0-578-76009-4 (digital edition)

For more information regarding special discounts for bulk purchases, please contact:

practialpurposesolutions@gmail.com

©Copyright 2021 Kendrea Robinson

ALL RIGHTS RESERVED
Printed in the U.S.A.

# Dedication

I dedicate this book to my daughter in heaven Samori Ellaree Fox, Gloria Moore, William Moore, and my grandmothers, Ellaree Moore and Helen Wragg. I would like to thank God for allowing me to have capabilities to produce this book. Most importantly, I am so grateful for my parents for instilling Prayer and Faith into my life as a child. To my grandma Ellaree: thank you for just being the voice of encouragement. No matter what I tell you I want to do, your first response is, "Do it. You can do anything you set your heart out to do." To my grandmother Helen, may you rest in peace for everything I do in health is for all that she endured. To my daughter, thank you for coming into my life the time you did to enlighten me on the lessons that were learned and the priceless moments that were gained. May she continue to rest in heaven angel.

# Foreword

Individuals throughout life tend to dream and envision so much for their lives. Sometimes these dreams require a certain level of achievement or involvement in a particular organization. This means that in order to accomplish that which the mind has set out to do, one needs to maintain balance in life. This balance starts with taking practical steps toward conquering these goals and being the best version of oneself. This means that in order to accomplish that which the mind has set out to do, one needs to maintain balance in life by continuously being married to self love.

Priorities can vary from individual to individual, and today I am here to remind you that you are a priority in your own life. I understand that you have many responsibilities, but you are your number one priority before anyone else. The definition of priority is what you make more essential than anything else. As you continue to read you will find out what life requires in order for you to be the best version of yourself. The first step towards achieving the vision you have set for yourself is knowing what your priorities are in your life. I am not talking about other individuals in your life but rather: what are your priorities for you before thinking about the tasks as a mother, father, daughter, sister or other titles you might hold?

Again, priorities will always vary from person to person. As you read this, I want you to ask yourself: how well am I prioritizing my life. The Maslow's Hierarchy of Needs generally states that we have and need to maintain the following needs, with each one building of the one before it: physiological, safety, love, esteem, and self-actualization. This means that we cannot reach self-actualization without meeting the needs that precede it. Once your most basic needs are met, I challenge you to take the journey of self-actualization, allowing God to guide you. I challenge you to hop on the journey of self actualization and being married to self.

# Contents

Ch. 1. Priorities — 13

Ch. 2. Protect YOUR Space — 21

Ch. 3. BETTER over Bitter — 25

Ch. 4. Time to Be Free — 29

Ch. 4 Embrace your Now — 36

CH. 5 No Time Wasting — 41

Ch. 6 Do Not Be Your Own Distraction — 45

Ch. 7 Tips to Maintaining the Balance — 48

Expressions of Gratitude — 52

# Priorities

*"Beloved, I wish above all things that thou mayest prosper and be in health, even as thy soul prospered." -3 John 1:2, King James Version*

In order to start the journey to making sure that your priorities are in proper alignment, you must begin with deciphering what you have made a priority before God and yourself. For example, to be anything to anybody else (i.e. a parent to a child, spouse to a significant other, or a caregiver to a loved one), you must try to do it with excellence. This requires you to be free of discomfort and full of positive energy, which leads to proper communication when your mental, emotional, and spiritual state is balanced. It is understandable that your children may keep you busy. The business is overwhelming and/ or the job's tasks are increasing, and by the time the day begins or ends, you are just tired. Yet, to reach your full potential and be successful and prosperous in your life you have got to make sure that your physical, mental, and emotional health are intact. If there are issues, you can find a way to manage them with the help of a healthcare professional that you can entrust.

If you are not making sure that your health is in alignment with what God wants for you, you will not be able to fully be the best version of yourself. Fulfilling this desire requires you to properly align your priorities. These priorities include your physical, mental, emotional, and spiritual health. Without acknowledging your need to be physically healthy, you may miss out on fully executing roles that you hold. For example, you cannot be involved in your child's life if you are always feeling tired or drained and lacking energy. The same goes for being a spouse. How can you properly enjoy your spouse with low energy due to health issues? Health is not only physical but also mental and emotional. We must ensure that we are mentally and emotionally stable if we ever hope to have productive relationships, even with ourselves. Here's a question to ponder: would your relationships be enjoyable if you were more mentally and emotionally stable?

If you are overweight, have a chronic condition, are continuously fatigue and tired, can you imagine what would happen if you create a change of lifestyle and pay closer attention to your physical health? There may even be individuals who are not aware that they have diabetes or high blood pressure. It may take them being rushed to the emergency room after having symptoms that never went away that lead to having a stroke or experiencing diabetic ketoacidosis (which is when the blood sugar is too high, and the patient is in a diabetic coma). These are extremes, but they remind us that we must "make time" for ourselves and our health. When we make the excuse that we do not have time to go to the doctor because we were feeling fine, must remind ourselves that we matter by choosing to learn what is going on in our bodies regardless of how scary it might feel.

**Tools and Tips to Properly Prioritizing a Healthy Lifestyle**

1. Perform a self-evaluation.

    a. What are my weaknesses that cause me to have an unhealthy lifestyle?

    _____

    _____

    _____

    _____

    _____

    _____

    _____

b. What are my strengths that cause me to live a healthy lifestyle?

_____

_____

_____

_____

_____

_____

_____

2. What am I putting before my health? (It is okay if your answer is "the family" and/or "job")How do I plan to prioritize and have a healthier lifestyle?

_____

_____

_____

_____
_____
_____
_____
_____

3. Which exercises will be doable for me? What days during the week will I be able to exercise and try to eat clean?

_____
_____
_____
_____
_____
_____
_____

4. What is or would be my motivation to keep me going?

   _____

   _____

   _____

   _____

   _____

   _____

   _____

5. How often will I weigh myself? What is my Long Term Goal (Months and Years)? What is my Short term Goal (Days and Weeks)?

   _____

   _____

   _____

   _____

## Protect YOUR Space

*"But the fruit of the Spirit is love, joy, peace, longsuffering, gentleness, goodness, faith, gentleness, self-control." -Galatians 5:22-23a*

Our assignment in life may give us individuals that we are specifically assigned to help. Many times, we can find ourselves loving individuals so deeply that their problems become our problems. That means we grasp hold of their issues and make it a priority to help them solve their problems while trying to manage our own personal problems. When taking another individual's responsibilities, we can become overwhelmed and neglect our own issues. This occurs because we have allowed someone to bring their problems into your space and nine times out of ten it was unintentional.

To keep life's balance and being married to self love, it is essential that we understand the importance of having boundaries within our lives, including your personal space to sustain proper love, joy, peace, patience, and kindness as requested by God. Who you invite into your space may determine how sustainable the Fruit of the Spirit are in your life. Be mindful of individuals who are always speaking negatively. Remember that negative thoughts and words can lie dormant in your life because it can lead to you thinking and or speaking negatively. This can also lead to disruption of your peace. Disruption of your peace can lead to you losing focus of your goals. This can also affect our relationships with other people because others may feel the negative energy or you may even begin to speak negatively to others. As you work to maintain your balance in life, I encourage you to protect your energy. Only allow people and things who will help contribute to your physical, mental, emotional, and spiritual health unless your giving to them is not affecting your personal space and peace. You must begin to decipher what is necessary for the next destination. I encourage you to write out what has been bothering you down below or on a separate sheet of paper. Tie it up and burn it after you have completed this task.

*I declare and decree that what is written down below will no longer disturb your peace. You understand that there is so much ahead of you. You cannot keep distractions on board. These things will no longer disrupt their peace. In Jesus' Name, Amen!*

**Write a list of the things that you are not carrying with you to the next destination:**

_____

_____

_____

_____

_____

_____

_____

# BETTER over Bitter

*"Let all bitterness, wrath, anger, clamor, and evil speaking be put away from you, with all malice. And be kind to one another, tenderhearted, forgiving one another, even as God in Christ forgave you." -Ephesians 4:31-32, New King James Version*

When something is considered bitter, it has a sharp or pungent taste. That goes for being a human being as well. When an individual is bitter, they may be described to be "sour acting," angry, and/or always negative when interacting with them. Being bitter leads to a place of unhappiness, which leads to a place of depression and or hopelessness. The world may seem to be caving in on you, causing you to begin to think negatively about yourself. When we start to think negatively about ourselves, it becomes difficult to think positively about anyone else. This may cause us to dive into a place of being uneasy and losing peace.

Don't allow bitterness to overtake your future. It will not only destroy your inner peace but also cause your bitter energy to be unattractive. Remember that bitterness WILL lead to physical and mental health damage over time. It can lead to depression, anxiety, hypertension, heart attacks, cancer, strokes, and even death. It is essential that we place ourselves in other people's shoes to understand how it feels if we wore the shoes they wear. Consider what it might feel like if you were on the receiving end of someone's bitter demeanor: I am sure that you wouldn't want to communicate with someone who is unfriendly and every time you converse with them they appear to have an unpleasant personality. The same is true for people who would encounter you in your bitterness.

    I cannot stress enough how important forgiveness is to our own healing. Unforgiveness is the breeding ground for bitterness. As you begin to practice forgiveness, this will allow you to begin to work on feeding your mind positivity in every situation. This practice will lead to persistent positivity in your daily living. Once you have reached the point of stepping into this newness, you must be consistent and unafraid to get help if you feel yourself converting back to consistent thoughts of the person that you've chosen to forgive. Bitterness prevents us from being successful, happy, healthy, and married to self love. You deserve to be balanced in life, and being balanced requires you to do it with peace, happiness, love, and joy.

**DO NOT BE BITTER, JUST BE BETTER!**

## Time to Be Free

*"Stand fast therefore in the liberty wherewith Christ hath made us free, and be not entangled with the yoke of bondage." -Galatians 5:1, King James Version*

We all want to live a life of freedom with no worries or stress. Unfortunately, worries and stress are a virtual certainty of life. Yet, you get to determine how you will manage the stress. In addition, don't forget that holding on to unforgiveness is being in bondage, which allows us to miss the promises that are for our lives. Being in bondage will lead to depression, anxiety, high blood pressure, and other chronic conditions such as diabetes, strokes, heart attacks, and more.

One clear example of turmoil that created bondage in my own life is when I lost my baby girl during childbirth. I remember going into premature labor around noon and not knowing exactly what was going on. All I knew was that it was a pain that I had never experienced in my life. As a nurse at the time so many thoughts ran across my mind. I drove from one hospital to the next, only to find that I was having contractions. By 9:00 p.m., I was birthing a baby girl after only having carried her for twenty-one weeks. From the first day of having nausea and vomiting and finding out I was pregnant to birthing her, I found a love on earth like never.

Ever been in bondage and didn't even realize it until you finally got out of bondage? I remember being pregnant for 21 weeks. The entire pregnancy was extremely uncomfortable, mentally, emotionally and physically. While I was pregnant it wasn't just about what my flesh wanted for me but what my flesh wanted for my child. My flesh wanted my child to experience having a father in her life as I did. I had to be accountable and understand that forcing myself in an unhealthy relationship due to our indifferences was not going to be a healthy decision.

The day I went into labor, it was the most excruciating pain I had ever felt. After delivering a little girl, I experienced a major release that I wasn't even aware I needed: twenty-one weeks, 147 days in bondage and not realizing it until after birthing her. I delivered a child that I would not have the chance to watch grow, but rather throwing myself into grief, I released the pain and decided to move forward.

I have been in bondage many times, and we all have. Some bondage is easier to get out of than others. There may be situations that arise that may warrant you to *run* out of bondage while other situations may cause you to slowly *crawl* or *walk* out of bondage that may take two, five, ten, or twenty years. Healing is oftentimes delayed because of our fear of the unknown. Healing is a scary process when you have become accustomed to pain.

You may have been molested, abused, or had to grow up faster than you wanted to. You may have even been a victim to prostitution at a young age. These situations do not have to hold you in bondage. Be free in knowing that your children will not be raised going through these situations. Be free in knowing that YOU MADE IT OUT. Be free in knowing that you did not die through the mess.

BE FREE, BE FREE, BE FREE. Below or in your personal journal, write out what has been holding you in bondage. Write it out, let the tears roll, think long and hard about all that you have been through. Release it down below or in your journal. After you write it out, pray this prayer: God, I thank you for allowing me to release this negative energy that has kept me in mental bondage. Thank you for allowing me to have the willpower to face what I've been through. Thank you for setting me free from this bondage that I have been in. I am going to move forward in freedom: freedom to be who you called me to be. I am no longer the same. After I release what has been keeping me in bondage, I will release the book, the dream, or whatever else you have in store for me to do. I am refocused. My mind and heart are renewed. The past no longer follows me. The future now has taken hold of me and my vision. In Jesus' Name, Amen!

_____

_____

_____

_____

_____

_____

_____

_____

_____

_____

_____

_____

_____

_____

_____

_____

Now you can move forward in peace and joy without going back and dwelling on it. It is all out of your system, and it is time to put in the work and stay here. **YOU ARE OFFICIALLY FREE FROM BONDAGE AND THERE IS NO TURNING BACK!**

## Embrace YOUR NOW

*"For I know the thoughts that I think toward you, saith the Lord, thoughts of peace, and not of evil, to give you an expected end." -Jeremiah 29:11, King James Version*

Now that you have accepted some of the issues that have been holding you back from becoming and being the best version of yourself, start to embrace your now today. Accepting that you have some new goals you want to conquer because you do not want to affect your health in the long run due to underlying preexisting conditions that can occur due to not putting yourself first.

As you work toward prioritizing and putting yourself first, start with embracing where you are now in life. Don't dwell on the fact that you might not be where you want to be but you are in the right place in life according to the plan of your life right now. Don't dwell on the fact that you might be where you want to be but you are in a place where you NEED to be. Remember the higher being is in control and if you do not stop dwelling on your wants and keep trying to take control over a life that was given to us by someone who already knows the plans for us you will continue to disappoint yourself. This leads to delay in your Purpose and sometimes it leads to never fulfilling your purpose.

You have dreams, goals, and a vision that you want to accomplish. As you go through the various roads in your lifelong journey to achieve that dream, goal, and/or vision, let me remind you that you will encounter life's offsets. This may lead to feelings of hopelessness, doubt, and maybe even fear. Today, I encourage you to think about all of life's offsets and how they have propelled you in many different ways.

During my own reflection, I recall my journey through college. In 2007, I went to college with a major in Nursing thinking that I had my life all planned out. I knew that I would be graduating and become a nurse by

2011. Unfortunately, I did not get accepted into the nursing program, and I took a detour, going back to my hometown to attend Florence Darlington Technical College (FDTC). With the help of God, I was able to complete the nursing program and graduate in 2012 after failing 2 classes while in the nursing program. Now I can look back and say that not getting accepted into the nursing program was one of my many offsets in life but it made me a better person.

According to Jeremiah 29:11, God knows the plans He has for our lives. He even knows the thoughts for your life. It all means that we must stop worrying and trust every one of life's offset. God has it designed to eventually work out for your benefit.

You may have found yourself writing the vision down with dates, time, places, and people not realizing at that time that those plans may change due to life offset. For example, such as the COVID-19 did, all those plans that I had for 2020 had to be canceled. This was a time that I had to realize that I had to recharge. I was able to refocus on keeping my mental, physical, and spiritual state intact. I was also able to utilize time that would have been spent out of the house being more productive. Sometimes God just wants you to recharge and the longer you sit still to charge, the longer your life battery will last.

No matter the offsets to life, find your balance mentally, physically, and spiritually and keep it. Do what is necessary to protect that balance that God has shown you is necessary for you to keep. Life may have some sticky situations, but you do not have to get stuck.

I encourage you to continue to be the best version of yourself despite Life offsets. Keep going despite the long nights you are staying up to study and create content. Keep going despite all the prayers YOU feel are being unanswered and the FASTING is not breaking anything through. Remember that your NOW is just as essential as your FUTURE. Without your PAST, there is no NOW, and without your NOW, there is no FUTURE.

## No Time Wasting

*"'Yes indeed, it won't be long now.' God's Decree. 'Things are going to happen so fast your head will swim, one thing fast on the heels of the other. You won't be able to keep up. Everything will be happening at once--and everywhere you look, blessings! Blessings like wine pouring off the mountains and hills. I'll make everything right again for my people. . .'"*
-Amos 9:13-15, The Message

So, get moving and push past your comfort zone. Of course, it is not going to be easy. You will have moments where you may want to quit, but you must keep pushing. Remember God is always placing individuals in our lives who will help us fulfill our purpose on this earth whether it's through motivation and/or services you can provide to them or vice versa. As you work to reach your full potential you are going to keep the balance. As you do this remember that **YOU DO NOT HAVE TIME TO**

**WASTE**. This means you do not have three months and five days to decide on when you are going to make the lifestyle change. Remember diseases have no wait time either. Remember the longer you wait on putting you first, you jeopardize your loved ones by not being WHOLE for them.

After giving birth to the little girl, I would never get the chance to raise and losing a person I thought I was going to share my life with; I recovered and decided to move forward from the pain of loss. To be more direct: I bounced back. Bouncing back will vary from individual to individual. For some that could mean taking a break from activities, people and not going certain places. For others that could be going to a psychiatrist, mental health counselor, pastor, personal trainer or getting a life coach for help and guidance. For some, all may be necessary to get to moving forward.

Three years later, I found myself in love with an amazing man. He came into my life and reminded me why I went through what I went through. The pain was indescribable: I lost my baby and had gone through a heartbreak due to my selfish gratification, but now I can tell God THANK YOU. I am grateful, however, for the pain because it helps me to cherish the people and things in my life with much more appreciation. Because I chose to focus on God's plan for my life, He shifted the trajectory of my life SUDDENLY. I encourage you today to stop wasting time in mediocrity and allow GOD to do BIGGER things in your life.

**Do NOT WASTE TIME!**

44

# Do Not Be Your Own Distraction

*"Have I not commanded thee? Be strong and courageous; be not afraid, neither be thou dismayed: for the Lord thy God is with thee whithersoever thou goest." -Joshua 1:9*

Remember the time you envisioned something without having the resources, the time, and/or the full commitment or desire to do it? That was the time that you were your own distraction. Many times we can doubt ourselves, which allows the universe in return to give us what we really don't want; however, because we envision NOT having what we dreamed to have after dreaming what we COULD have.

In order, to do anything in life, one must be conscious of themselves and their capabilities. As we travel this journey of life, make the conscious effort to decide that with every great idea we choose to do it with FAITH rather than FEAR. Choosing faith will ALWAYS allow you to jump over the hurdle of FEAR. Holding on to FEAR can cause so many ideas to just sit and wither away. Leaving the world to continue to wait on the solution to a problem. Do not be a victim and choose FEAR over FAITH.

Down Below Write your Fears down and Conquer them. Do what is necessary to get rid of the weight called FEAR!

My Fears:

_____

_____

_____

_____

_____

_____

## TAKE FAITH OVER FEAR!!!

## Tips to Maintaining the Balance

**Physical:**

- Maintain an Exercise Routine.
- Make Healthy Food Choices.
- Manage chronic conditions that you may have such as diabetes, hypertension, chronic kidney disease, asthma, chronic obstructive pulmonary disease (COPD).
- Keep your annual Exams.
- Keep Follow up Appointments.
- Follow through with any consults your provider has recommended.
- Don't let symptoms slip away, if it doesn't feel right it is okay to seek medical attention for further evaluation. If you are not content, always seek for a second opinion from another physician. Just like you shop around for a certain shoe, shirt

and or house, the same applies for the provider you get medical advice from.

- Detox Approximately and timely.

**Mental:**

- Forgive
- Maintain ONLY HEALTHY RELATIONSHIPS
- SAY NO to people, places, and things that are not beneficial to your mental health.
- Find a place of relief.
- Go to mental health counseling, finding a safe space to voice your feelings and being able to receive advice that will be beneficial for you.
- Surround yourself around like-minded individuals or individuals who have the attributes you want to obtain in the future.
- Meditate
- ALWAYS RELAX, REST and REST.
- Find time to reprocess events good and bad to strategize your future wants, needs and do not

want and do not need.

- Know when to be still (This means knowing when not to work on the business, when not to go places, when not answering the phone and or text).
- Know when to detox from people who are draining you.

**<u>Emotional Health</u>**
- Don't worry about things that have not happened.
- Keep a smile on your face even when you don't want to.
- Always be thankful for the Good and Bad.
- Do not just say you let Go but actually Let Go.
- Detox from social media if it starts to make you feel competitive, sad or behind.
- Delete individuals who bring negative thoughts to your mind and make you gossip when on and or off social media.

**<u>Spiritual:</u>**
- Maintain FAITH over FEAR.

- Seek spiritual guidance from someone who can help guide you to a better relationship with God.

- Create and maintain a prayer life.

- Go on a fast.

- Let Go and Let God.

**To keep the Balance in your Mental, Physical, Emotional and Spiritual State of Life you must ALWAYS:**

- Reprocess
- Regroup
- Rest
- Refocus

# Expressions of Gratitude

Dear Reader,

Thank you for taking the time to read, <u>Married to Self Love</u>. May this book change your life forever and give you a greater insight on how to love YOU again. May you now be able to prioritize your life by making sure that you are whole, not some days, but all the days of your life. It may be challenging but it is worth it! Now go on and continue to love YOU, despite how productive your life may be and or how you feel. Activate Self Love like never before.

*Thank you,*

*Kendrea Robinson, FNP-C*

www.ingramcontent.com/pod-product-compliance
Lightning Source LLC
Chambersburg PA
CBHW071416290426
44108CB00014B/1846